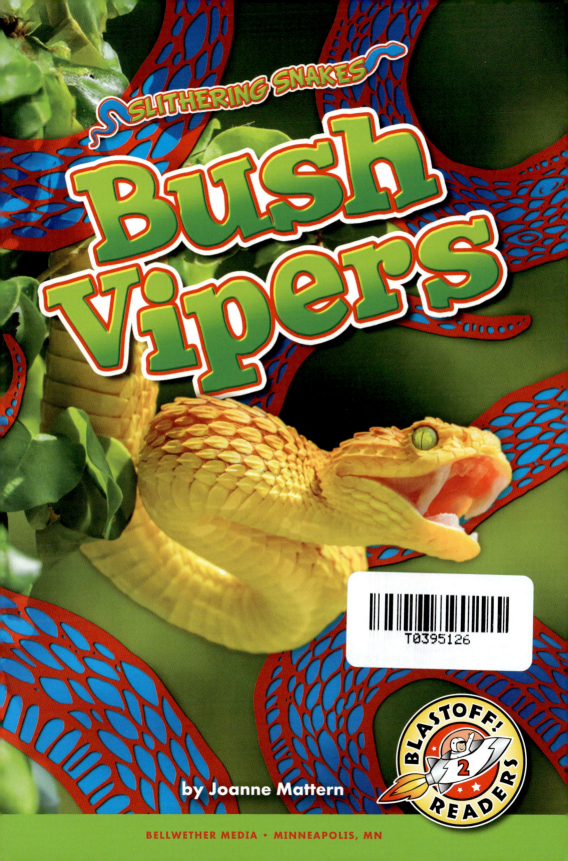

Slithering Snakes

Bush Vipers

by Joanne Mattern

BELLWETHER MEDIA • MINNEAPOLIS, MN

Blastoff! Readers are carefully developed by literacy experts to build reading stamina and move students toward fluency by combining standards-based content with developmentally appropriate text.

Level 1 provides the most support through repetition of high-frequency words, light text, predictable sentence patterns, and strong visual support.

Level 2 offers early readers a bit more challenge through varied sentences, increased text load, and text-supportive special features.

Level 3 advances early-fluent readers toward fluency through increased text load, less reliance on photos, advancing concepts, longer sentences, and more complex special features.

★ **Blastoff! Universe**

Reading Level

Grade K

Grades 1–3

Grade 4

This edition first published in 2026 by Bellwether Media, Inc.

No part of this publication may be reproduced in whole or in part without written permission of the publisher. For information regarding permission, write to Bellwether Media, Inc., Attention: Permissions Department, 3500 American Blvd W, Suite 150, Bloomington, MN 55431.

Library of Congress Cataloging-in-Publication Data

LC record for Bush Vipers available at: https://lccn.loc.gov/2025001564

Text copyright © 2026 by Bellwether Media, Inc. BLASTOFF! READERS and associated logos are trademarks and/or registered trademarks of Bellwether Media, Inc. Bellwether Media is a division of FlutterBee Education Group.

Editor: Kieran Downs   Designer: Brittany McIntosh

Printed in the United States of America, North Mankato, MN.

Table of Contents

Small But Deadly	4
On the Hunt	12
Bush Viper Babies	18
Glossary	22
To Learn More	23
Index	24

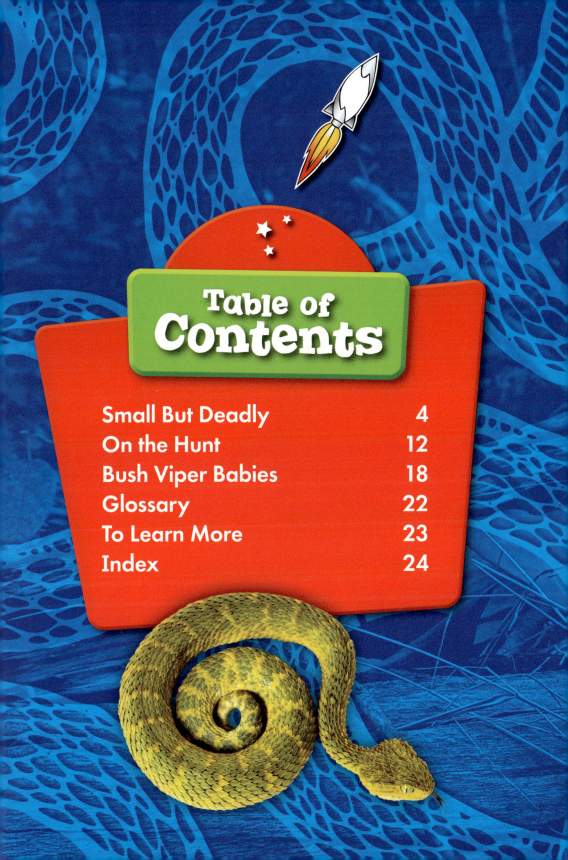

Small But Deadly

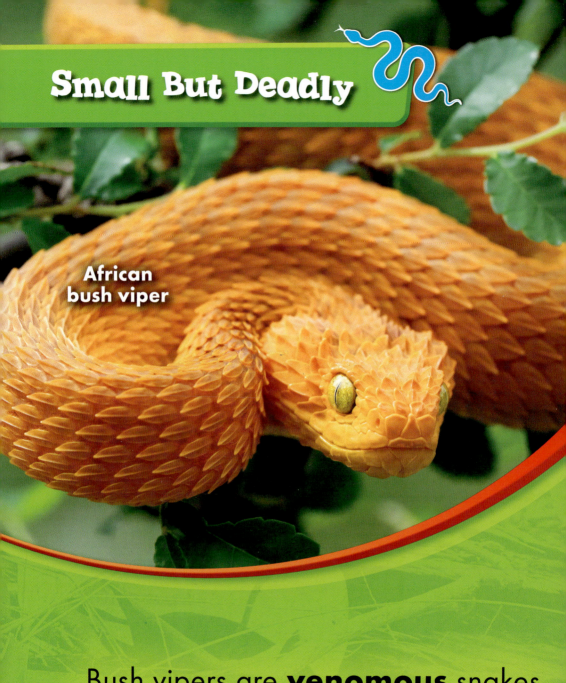

African bush viper

Bush vipers are **venomous** snakes. There are 18 different **species** of bush vipers.

These **reptiles** live in western and central Africa.

African Bush Viper Range

range =

Bush vipers are small snakes. They can grow to be up to 3 feet (0.9 meters) long.

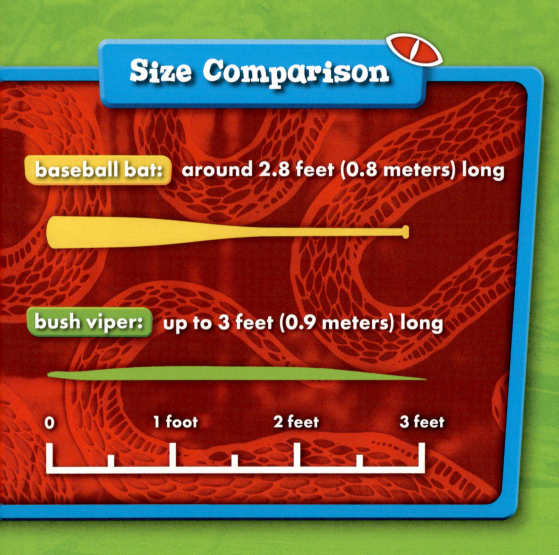

These snakes weigh up to 8 pounds (3.6 kilograms).

Bush vipers come in many different colors. Some have spots.

Bush vipers have **scales** that curl on the edges.

curled scales

African hairy bush viper

Bush vipers have a **prehensile** tail. The tail curls around tree branches.

Their large eyes sit at the front of their triangle-shaped heads.

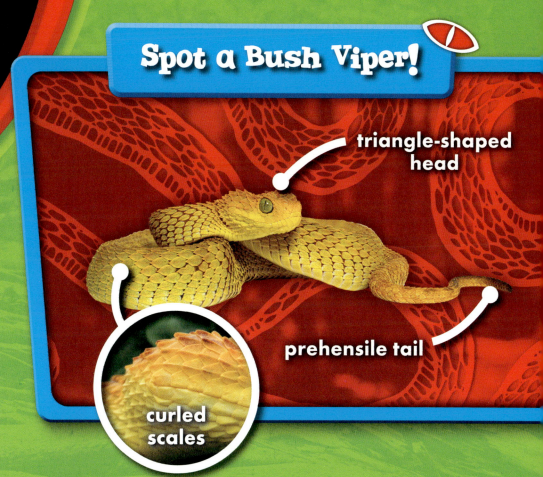

Spot a Bush Viper!

triangle-shaped head

prehensile tail

curled scales

On the Hunt

Bush vipers live in **rain forests**. They hunt at night.

They hang from low branches and wait for **prey**. When prey gets too close, bush vipers attack!

Bush Viper Food

African dwarf frogs

common agamas

four-toed elephant shrews

fangs

Bush vipers eat **rodents**, birds, and lizards. The snakes bite their prey with their sharp **fangs**.

Their venom quickly finishes off prey.

Many animals eat bush vipers. These snakes are in danger from large **mammals**, birds, and other snakes.

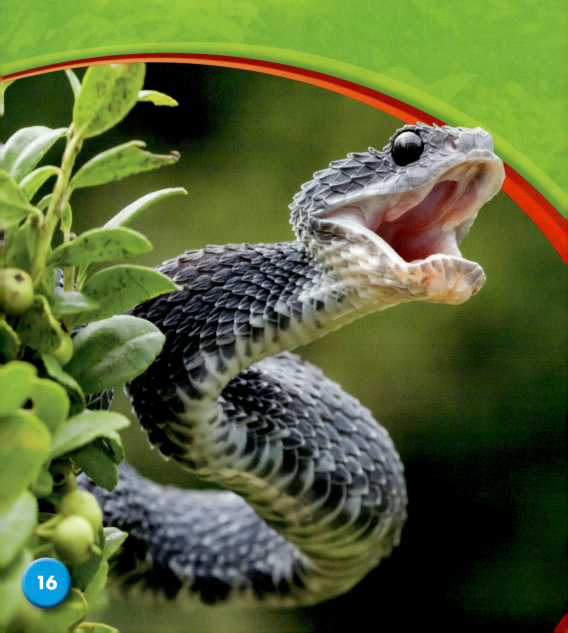

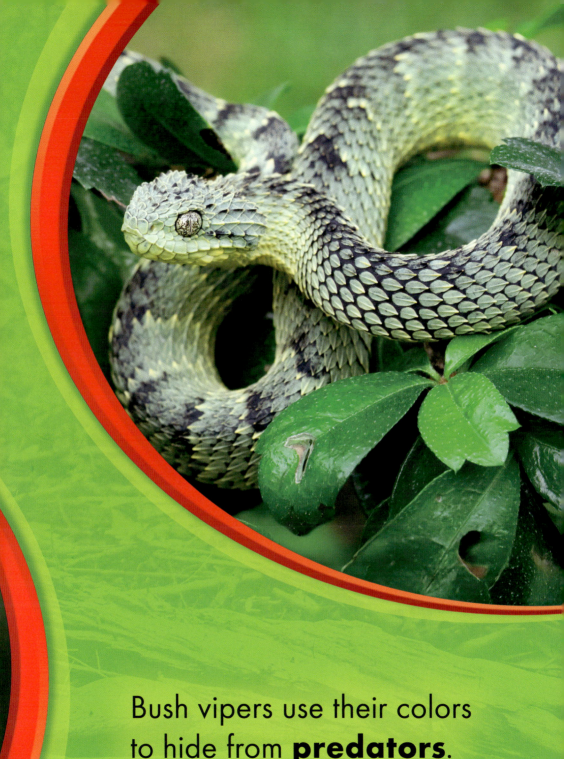

Bush vipers use their colors to hide from **predators**.

Bush Viper Babies

Most snakes lay eggs.
Not bush vipers!

These snakes give birth to live babies. They have 9 to 12 babies at a time.

Bush viper babies take care of themselves right after birth.

They like to live alone. In time, the snakes will have their own babies!

African Bush Viper Stats

status in the wild: least concern

life span: up to 20 years

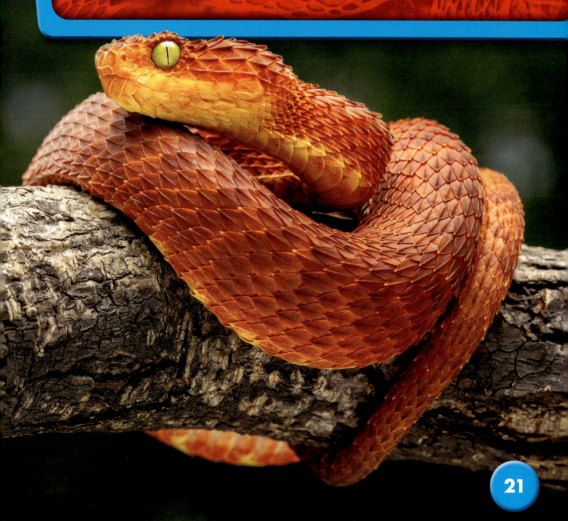

Glossary

fangs—long, sharp teeth

mammals—warm-blooded animals that have backbones and feed their young milk

predators—animals that hunt other animals for food

prehensile—able to grab onto something

prey—animals that are hunted by other animals for food

rain forests—thick, green forests that receive a lot of rain

reptiles—cold-blooded animals that have backbones and usually lay eggs

rodents—small animals that gnaw on their food

scales—plates that cover an animal's body

species—types of an animal

venomous—able to produce venom; venom is a kind of poison made by some snakes.

To Learn More

AT THE LIBRARY

Davies, Monika. *Deadly Vipers*. New York, N.Y.: Gareth Stevens, 2023.

Nguyen, Suzane. *Copperheads*. Minneapolis, Minn.: Bellwether Media, 2025.

Rose, Rachel. *Bush Viper*. Minneapolis, Minn.: Bearport Publishing, 2025.

ON THE WEB

FACTSURFER

Factsurfer.com gives you a safe, fun way to find more information.

1. Go to www.factsurfer.com.

2. Enter "bush vipers" into the search box and click 🔍.

3. Select your book cover to see a list of related content.

Index

Africa, 5
alone, 20
babies, 19, 20
bite, 14
colors, 8, 17
eyes, 11
fangs, 14
food, 13, 14
heads, 11
hide, 17
hunt, 12
night, 12
predators, 16, 17
prey, 12, 14, 15
rain forests, 12
range, 5
reptiles, 5
scales, 9, 11
size, 6, 7
species, 4
spots, 8

stats, 21
tail, 10, 11
venomous, 4, 15

The images in this book are reproduced through the courtesy of: Mark_Kostich, front cover, pp. 4, 9, 11 (inset), 12-13, 14, 15, 17, 18, 19, 20; Eric Isselee, pp. 3, 11, 22; Mark Kostich, pp. 7, 8, 12, 16; Roger de la Harpe, p. 10; Guillermo Guerao Serra, p. 13 (frog); Nick Greaves, p. 13 (shrew); Nina B, p. 13 (agama); Lauren Suryanata, pp. 20-21.